A CAREER AS A
TEACHER

Annalise Silivanch

ROSEN
PUBLISHING

NEW YORK

For Ella and Lena:
I hope the classrooms of today and tomorrow nurture your whole selves.

Published in 2011 by The Rosen Publishing Group, Inc.
29 East 21st Street, New York, NY 10010

Library of Congress Cataloging-in-Publication Data

Silivanch, Annalise.
A career as a teacher / Annalise Silivanch.—1st ed.
   p. cm.—(Essential careers)
Includes bibliographical references and index.
ISBN 978-1-4358-9468-6 (library binding)
1. Education—Vocational guidance—United States—Juvenile literature. 2. Teaching—Vocational guidance—United States—Juvenile literature. I. Title.
LB2831.58.S56 2011
371.10023'73—dc20

2009044971

Manufactured in the United States of America

CPSIA Compliance Information: Batch #S10YA: For Further Information Contact Rosen Publishing, New York, New York at 1-800-237-9932

contents

INTRO

Teachers can help their students gain perspective on the larger world and their place in it.

DUCTION

Teachers play an important role in helping children grow in curiosity, knowledge, skills, and confidence. A good teacher can help a child meet his or her goals and find success. Teachers can help students enjoy learning and create a strong school spirit. Even in a recession, schools need teachers to organize and lead classes for young people. A teaching career can last for decades and allow one to grow into a confident educational leader.

The best teachers are helpful, interesting people who like to present information in fresh and exciting ways. Many teachers find the career rewarding because they can see some of their impact on students happen before their eyes. Some students return to visit and talk with their favorite teachers, sharing their successes and asking for advice. Teachers help shape the values, perspectives, and work ethic of the next generation.

Traditional teachers work within schools designed for different age groups: preschool, elementary school, middle school, and high school. Each teaching level has its own advantages and challenges. Young children need teachers to help them learn basic academic skills and appropriate school behavior. Teenagers may require someone to motivate and inspire them. All levels require energy, creativity, and a high level of organization.

Teachers quickly learn that the job requires more than just sharing information. A teacher often has to go "above and beyond" to help students achieve. That may mean spending extra time or coaching students through personal problems.

Today's teachers work in schools that are increasingly diverse, with more students for whom English is a second language. Teacher training now gives teachers strategies to help these students succeed.

Today's teachers strive to combine lectures and visual lessons with discussions, group problem-solving activities, and computer-based learning.

Ideas about teaching and learning have changed. Today, successful teachers are good public speakers and instructors, but they also help students take charge of their own learning. To accomplish this, they design activities that children can do in an active, hands-on way, such as group explorations, problem-solving exercises, computer-based lessons, or classroom games. Some teachers incorporate music, art, and other creative approaches into their learning material.

Whether they are teaching an academic subject or leading a club, sports team, or study hall, teachers with creativity and a positive attitude can inspire students. When a child grows up and looks back, a great teacher can be one of the treasures of his or her life.

chapter 1

THE BASICS OF TEACHING

Teachers are usually drawn to the career by a love of learning and an interest in helping students enjoy learning, too. Teaching is a "helping" profession—one that allows a person to use his or her mind and imagination. A teacher has the opportunity to present lessons in a fresh, original way. So a person who enjoys a creative challenge can make an excellent teacher. A teacher does much more than simply present information. A teacher thinks on his or her feet, reacting to and working with the spirit of the students in the room. A good teacher cares whether students learn and feels satisfied when they do. Even many years into their careers, most teachers continue to enjoy their work. In fact, according to a 2007 study by the National Center for Education Statistics, 93 percent of teachers who had been teaching for ten years said they were satisfied with their jobs.

TEACHING IS STABLE

Traditionally, teaching has been seen as a stable job. While schools are not immune from economic downturns, public schools with many students do not close overnight. Public schools are supported by taxpayer dollars. If a town's school board decides to make big changes to the school budget, taxpayers usually have the opportunity to approve it or reject it. Teachers usually get

Polls find that a majority of teachers enjoy their jobs, even many years after they begin teaching.

plenty of notice about changes, such as in the spring of the previous school year. Further, public schools guarantee a level of security for teachers and administrators who have shown themselves to be capable. After several years of working successfully in a school district, you can be eligible for tenure, or protection from suddenly being fired. Private schools and charter schools are subject to different rules and may offer less job security.

Looking ahead, more jobs are expected for new teachers as the overall U.S. population continues to grow and as schools continue to set new goals for academic achievement. Also, many experienced teachers are expected to retire and new teachers will be needed to replace them. A government forecast on the growth of teaching jobs estimates average-to-good growth. However, given the sheer number of schools, this growth likely means hundreds of thousands of new jobs.

A TEACHER'S SALARY

A teacher can make a modest-to-good income, depending on where he or she works. A teacher's salary usually depends on the state's cost of living, or how much it costs to pay for housing and other basic needs. For instance, the average teacher's salary in California for the 2007–2008 school year was nearly $30,000 above the average salary in South Dakota, which paid the lowest salary in the country. Where it costs more to live, teachers typically get a boost in income.

A teacher's salary also depends on years of experience in the classroom. Most public school districts have a set salary scale. Teachers with the same number of years of work experience are typically paid the same amount. However, extra academic credentials can boost a teacher's salary. A teacher with a master's or doctoral degree, or with multiple certifications, can see increased pay.

About half of all U.S. teachers belong to a union. A union is a work association that bargains for a salary and benefits for its members. Unions also bargain for limits to work hours and days and push for better working conditions in schools. Preschool teachers and private school teachers are less likely to belong to a union than public school teachers.

Above a standard salary, teachers have a number of ways they can earn extra money. Some are paid to coach extracurricular sports teams or work with an after-school club. They might help with production of the school play or work as part of a school-based tutoring club. Teachers might serve as summer school instructors or have a summer job. Many teachers develop a side career that they can pursue during weekends, summers, and school breaks.

For information on current teachers' salaries, refer to the Bureau of Labor Statistics' *Occupational Outlook Handbook* (http://www.bls.gov/oco) or the Web site of the National Education Association (http://www.nea.org).

Options in Teaching, Pre-K to 12

Teachers have different job descriptions, depending on the grade level they teach. In early education classes, teachers act more as guides while children adjust to the social rules of school. Elementary teachers help students develop basic skills in reading, writing, and mathematics. In middle school, teachers help students focus on learning while peer pressure rises around them. In high school, students are starting to discover and develop their talents, and an encouraging teacher can help them do this. A teacher's own education, experiences, and personality may help define what age group and subject matter he or she would prefer to teach.

EARLY EDUCATION

Teachers who work with the youngest students (preschool and kindergarten) typically have their own classrooms and work with the same group of students for the entire year. Early education teachers work hard to design their classrooms with young students in mind. The classroom will usually have areas for different activities: a play area, a quiet reading area, a "circle" area (where students can sit as a group for a lesson or song), and an area of desks or tables for academic work or art.

At the preschool level, a typical day is structured in small sections of time (sometimes only fifteen minutes) with activities that change often. Education at this level is more social than academic: students practice taking turns, raising their hands to speak, and working together. Students also

Early education students learn best in colorful classrooms with lots of different activities. Teachers help children practice social skills, like sharing and patience, and motor skills, like cutting and writing.

work on skills in preparation for elementary academics. For example, children develop motor skills through painting or sand play. Early language skills are taught through stories, games, and songs. Introductory math and science skills are involved in counting, building, and nature exploration. Dance, music, and all kinds of art are often used to stimulate young learners.

In the past, kindergarten classes were play-based, half-day programs that were similar to preschool. However, that has changed in the last few decades. Concerns about children's academic readiness and the need for parents to work have caused schools to develop more academic, full-day programs. Most school districts house kindergarten programs within their elementary schools. Kindergarten teachers now instruct children in phonics (connecting letters to sounds) and early math (recognizing patterns, counting, and doing simple addition). The kindergarten curriculum also includes music, social studies, science, and even computers. In a full-day kindergarten classroom, teachers plan a day that allows for the natural rhythms of snacks, lunch, and rest time along with lessons and activities.

More than ever, children are enrolled in early education programs. School districts are concerned about students reading levels and standardized test scores. Early education seems to prepare children for reading and math earlier. These programs should continue to grow as long as local and state education boards can fund them.

ELEMENTARY SCHOOL

After the shift to academic work in kindergarten, the elementary school teacher's instructional role in the classroom expands. Actual teaching time increases as children's attention spans do, and the subject matter becomes more complex.

Most classroom teachers in first through sixth grade teach a number of basic academic subjects—including math, reading, writing, and social studies—to the same group of students. The children typically have additional teachers for music, art, library/media, computer science, and physical education. Some schools also offer foreign languages. Some districts have moved sixth graders up to middle school to join seventh and eighth graders, while other school districts have found success by instructing sixth graders in their own school.

Elementary school teachers, like early education teachers, may find it rewarding to spend a whole year watching the same group of students grow and learn. They may find one year's class—with all of its individual personalities—to be entirely different from last year's. Elementary teachers strive to meet the academic needs of all of the children in the class, including higher- and lower-achieving students. This may mean finding time to lead several reading and math groups working at different levels. The amount of time invested in encouraging children can forge a lasting bond, with many students returning to hug their favorite former teacher.

In order to enjoy a good year, teachers at this level try to establish classroom rules and habits right away. When they do, students are clear about what rewards they may receive for cooperation and what penalties are given for bad behavior.

When a teacher clearly defines rules and expectations for classroom behavior and performance, students know what is expected of them.

MIDDLE SCHOOL AND HIGH SCHOOL

In middle school and high school, most teachers specialize in teaching one academic subject, such as history, English,

High school teachers specialize in the subjects they teach, and they may also lead an extracurricular arts, sports, or academic group.

or Spanish, to many different classes. Teachers need to complete sufficient course work, such as a college major, in the subject they teach. They must also take education courses in which they learn methods for teaching the subject. Each subject teacher might also have a homeroom class, or a group of students who begin or end the day in the class, for attendance, announcements, and other guidance.

In high school, music (vocal and instrumental) and art classes are often part of a student's week. Also, students typically find many extracurricular clubs, sports teams, and performing arts groups to join after school. Teachers who are paid to lead these groups usually enjoy the chance to work with students outside the classroom and share their expertise in an area of interest.

SPECIAL SUBJECTS AND SERVICES

A school depends on its specialized teachers to "round out" a child's education with art, music, instrumental music, physical education, and vocational classes. A specialized arts teacher receives his or her training in that particular art form or skill, but also learns teaching methods and techniques.

Special subject teachers help students learn in different, but no less valuable, ways than regular classroom teachers do. Special subject teachers can play an important role in a student's education. A child who has a hard time focusing in reading may be the same child who comes to life in a music class. Another child who gets discouraged by math might be a gifted athlete in gym. As for the teachers, they often enjoy the variety that comes from working with children in many different age groups. They may also work with some of the same students from year to year.

Special education teachers play a unique role in a school. Special education teachers serve students with learning disabilities, physical disabilities, and other special needs. Working with children whose disabilities range from mild to severe, special education teachers bring extra training to their jobs. The students they work with may have a variety of learning issues. Students may have learning disabilities such as dyslexia, hearing or speech disabilities, emotional disturbances, or autism, just to name a few. Teachers who work with these students use special teaching methods and techniques to help them learn. Because of the demands of this job, many states require special education teachers to have a master's degree in the field.

Teaching jobs in special education are actually growing at a faster rate than regular teaching jobs. This rise comes as

High school music teachers help students bring practice, attention, and determination to the skill of music performance.

SUBSTITUTE TEACHING

When a full-time teacher is absent, school districts call upon a roster of substitute teachers. Substitutes usually work "on call" at one or more schools and grade levels, and can be called the very morning they are needed. They may be hired to cover longer teacher absences as well. Substitute teachers are paid only for the days they work, so there is no regular, dependable salary. In addition, substitutes can often be the teachers that students like to pick on, since they believe they can get away with it. The absent teacher may or may not leave a lesson plan for the day. A substitute needs to be resourceful and think on his or her feet to create fun and educationally relevant activities.

Substitute teachers come from all backgrounds: a semiretired individual who enjoys the school environment, a parent returning to work part-time, or a college graduate who is seeking a job in that school district. Substituting is a great way to share an enthusiasm for learning and people.

more children are screened for disabilities earlier in life in order to get them the help they need. Evidence has shown that children whose learning difficulties are identified and addressed early have more success in school and in the future. In addition, federal laws require that students who need special services in school receive them. In many areas of the country, there is a shortage of teachers who are trained in special education. As a result, teachers with the required training are in high demand.

chapter 2

THE RHYTHMS OF THE CLASSROOM

Over the course of just one school year, a teacher can make a huge difference in the lives of his or her students. For example, when working with young children, a teacher can help them explore new ideas and share them with others. A teacher also helps open up the gift of literacy for children. "There's nothing more rewarding than teaching kindergarten," says teacher Kathy Fitzpatrick. "Imagine a child who can barely grasp a pencil entering your classroom in September. Then imagine that same child leaving your classroom in June, writing stories." When teaching older children, a teacher can help students discover and develop their unique talents. These changes can occur over a series of regular school days, weeks, and months. But how do teachers divide up a school day of six or more hours to help students reach important goals?

A TYPICAL DAY: ELEMENTARY SCHOOL

Each school day is organized with time for academics, lunch, recess, snack breaks, and special classes, like art and gym. An elementary school teacher prepares ahead of time by planning what content the day's lessons will cover and coming up with related activities. This preparation also includes finding or

A good elementary school teacher coaches students to develop new skills and gives them regular feedback on their efforts.

creating books, worksheets, visual displays, and other materials for each lesson. Math and language study take up the most teaching time, especially because these two areas make up annual standardized tests.

During the course of the day, students spend time as a group learning with the teacher and spend time doing independent work. As students complete assignments, the teacher monitors their progress and helps children individually as needed. Teachers may also allow students free time in the classroom to explore learning centers or read independently. During some periods, teachers may divide the class into smaller groups based on students' skill levels in a subject. Then they lead lessons geared to the needs of each group.

The day's lessons also include some science, geography, and history, or all of these combined in some way. As an example, a class study of Native Americans can include nearly every subject and some hands-on craft projects. Such a unit can reach students of all different learning styles.

As students leave the classroom for lunch or other classes, a teacher may have some time for lesson preparation, grading, or communication with parents. Or, they may be scheduled to supervise children in the cafeteria or on the playground. Near the end of the school day, teachers spend time explaining homework assignments to the students. Once students are dismissed for the day, the teacher still has lots of work ahead: grading, preparing worksheets and reading materials for the next day, making notes about students' behavior and progress, and cleaning up the classroom. A school may also schedule after school meetings or professional development (extra training for teachers) with faculty and supervisors. This can make for a long day. Many teachers don't leave until 5 PM after arriving at school by 7:30 AM or earlier.

SAMPLE DAILY SCHEDULE OF AN ELEMENTARY SCHOOL TEACHER

An elementary teacher's day is a busy one. The day is packed with activities, and there is little time to take a break from supervising students. The following is a sample schedule for a typical day:

7:15   Arrive; get coffee.

7:30   Attend early meeting. Complete any last-minute preparations.

8:00   Students arrive, unpack, and complete the "morning challenge" or "problem of the day."

8:10   Class recites the Pledge of Allegiance.

8:15   Hold a morning meeting with the class: take attendance; do lunch count; make announcements; review notes from home. Students share personal news briefly.

8:25   Teach language arts/writing lesson.

9:00   Walk students to library, computer science, art, or physical education. Review daily tasks with teacher's assistant (if teacher has one), mark papers, and prepare for upcoming lessons.

9:40   Teach reading lesson.

10:20 Ten-minute snack/recess.

10:30 Teach math lesson.

11:15 Teach spelling lesson/lead spelling game.

11:40 Lunch/recess (may share lunch duty with another teacher); take twenty-minute break.

12:30 Students do independent reading or work at learning centers.

1:00   Teach social studies lesson.

1:40	Teach science lesson.
2:20	Explain homework. School chorus takes a few students out of class; remaining students work together as teams on a project.
2:35	Quick game, if time permits.
2:40	Have students clean up and pack up for dismissal. Dismiss students to appropriate parents, caregivers, or the bus.
3:00	Hold a parent conference (when necessary); mark papers; answer phone calls and e-mails; get ready for the next day's activities. Decorate bulletin boards. Straighten up desk and classroom.
By 5:00	Leave the school, bringing any unfinished work to complete at home.

A TYPICAL DAY: MIDDLE AND HIGH SCHOOL

Teachers at the middle and high school levels interact with more students for a smaller amount of time. The school day is broken up into units of instruction that might last for one or two periods. As a result, teachers need to get in and out of lessons quickly and smoothly and build the subject a little each day. Concepts are explored in more depth at this level, and teachers create more tests and writing assignments to measure students' progress. Because secondary teachers are trained in their subjects, they are expected to be good sources of information.

The schedules of middle and high schools tend to build in more breaks for teachers. Some schools give teachers a prep period during the day devoted to grading, lecture preparation, and other tasks. During free periods, a teacher may also be assigned to monitor a study hall or homeroom.

THE LURE OF SUMMERS OFF

When discussing a career as a teacher, many people cite the perk of summers off. Most teachers in the United States receive the traditional two-month break after a ten-month

During the summer break, many teachers work with young people in recreational settings or summer school.

school year. While some people consider such a schedule to be a luxury, many teachers believe it is a necessity to take a break from the intensity of school. Philadelphia-area teacher Anna Weiss, writing for the *Philadelphia Public School Notebook*, points out that the summer break may be the only way some teachers avoid career burnout. "I personally work about sixty to seventy hours a week," she says. "It's more than I'm contracted to work, but I willingly do it because in teaching, it's just a given that you're going to work outside of the school day."

Teachers use the time off in different ways. For example, many teachers work a second job to bring in additional income. While some decide to exercise completely different skills during the summertime, others directly apply their teaching skills to positions as tutors, summer-session instructors, or camp staffers. Many teachers use the time off to do professional development, attending summer courses or conferences that will help them improve their teaching. Instead of working or studying, other teachers may travel or spend time with their families.

However, the traditional teaching schedule may be changing. Some schools have shifted to (or

Bringing Students Up to Standards

Since 2001, U.S. federal law has required public schools to show that all students are meeting academic standards. Schools must show that students are doing reading, writing, and math work at the appropriate grade level, as measured by state tests.

How does this affect the rhythms of the classroom? In many places, especially in urban areas, teachers are required to spend a large portion of the day on reading and math or assigning work that looks similar to the test. As even kindergarten classes dive into academic work, some students do well with the increased test prep time, and others do not. Since so much time must be spent preparing for standardized tests, some teachers find they need to eliminate other topics, projects, and ways of learning. As fifth-grade teacher John Shapiro says, "The interesting, creative aspect of being a student today is lost because districts are so worried about passing the test."

In addition, teachers say they feel pressure for all of their students to succeed on these tests, regardless of any learning issues students may have. "Today, teachers are expected to meet higher performance standards and to teach increasingly diverse students with different learning styles, learning disabilities and limited English proficiency," writes Barnet Berry of the Center for Teaching Quality. School test results are now widely published online and in newspapers, and they can affect the status of schools as well as the amount of government money schools receive. As a result, the worry of administrators can trickle down to teacher supervisors and then to teachers themselves.

It's unlikely that student tests will disappear anytime soon. By 2009, the federal government was asking states to include student test scores in evaluating teachers. If anything, teachers may be judged in the future more strictly than ever. They may need to demonstrate innovation and student achievement at the same time. The good news? High-energy, creative teachers that motivate their students with high expectations may be rewarded more than in the past. A number of school districts are starting to experiment with merit-based systems. These new programs give teachers extra pay if their students show significant progress or improvement.

will shift to) a year-round schedule with regular breaks. This new schedule is more common in urban areas. Educators have found that the constant structure prevents "summer learning loss" and removes some of the risks to children that an unstructured summer might bring. In 2009, Secretary of Education Arne Duncan said he would push for more schools to try the year-round model so American students can better compete with students from other countries.

Despite the pressure on teachers to cover material, they can help create a fun and supportive environment in a school.

chapter 3

WHO IS A GOOD TEACHER?

Whatsort of person makes a good teacher? In 2005, the *College Student Journal* found that personality traits probably had the biggest influence over whether a new teacher stayed with and enjoyed the career. It is important that teachers enjoy and connect with their work, since that can help motivate an entire school full of students, other teachers, and administrators.

PERSONAL QUALITIES

A teacher with passion and creativity makes the classroom come alive with ideas, discussion, and engaging activities. The qualities of patience and cooperation create a peaceful place for learning, free of conflict. Energy and enthusiasm are also important: A teacher needs to find a way to motivate students who may be tired, distracted, or discouraged. Organization is key for planning lessons and grading papers. Finally, teachers may need authority most of all because if students don't respect a teacher's guidelines, no learning can take place.

Different grade levels require different personalities, or at least an ability to change one's approach. Preschool and kindergarten students feel safe in an unfamiliar environment if their teacher is understanding and caring. Fifth graders appreciate a

A good teacher inspires students to think deeply, ask questions, and become involved with the world around them.

little wackiness from a creative teacher, since they are beginning to plug into their own talents and confidence. Middle and high school students will admire a teacher who leads the class with respectful authority, but also brings humor into the classroom.

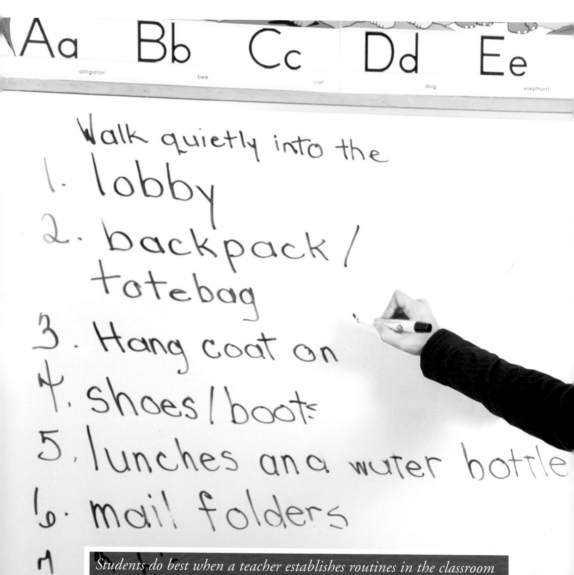

Aa   Bb   Cc   Dd   Ee

alligator   bee   cat   dog   elephant

Walk quietly into the
1. lobby
2. backpack / totebag
3. Hang coat on
4. shoes / boots
5. lunches and a water bottle
6. mail folders
7.

Students do best when a teacher establishes routines in the classroom and practices them with the class.

IMPORTANT TEACHING SKILLS

While being a "people" person is helpful, a teacher-in-training also develops and practices the specific teaching skills needed in the classroom.

An effective teacher must plan a course of study appropriate to an age group and then manage the class's attention and interest. A teacher evaluates each student's understanding of concepts and his or her social and emotional functioning in the classroom. Finally, a teacher needs to get along with and share ideas with other teachers, as well as communicate with parents and welcome their questions. Over time, teachers learn the best ways to approach the challenges in each area.

CLASSROOM MANAGEMENT

Keeping a classroom of students focused is no small job. Each child brings his or her own feelings and energy levels to the group. Children may be tired, hungry, stressed, excited, restless, or even angry. They may be resisting the very idea of being in school that day.

To bring a level of focus, teachers need to create a clear structure in a classroom. In elementary school, teachers give a certain rhythm to the day. They do this by setting up a daily schedule to help the classroom run smoothly. These routines help students get involved in each learning activity and behave appropriately. Routines also help signal the beginning and end of each activity. In older grades, this structure becomes more academic in nature. For example, there may be a certain pace to projects and a certain day each week for quizzes.

Children, like adults, work best when there is a goal. As a result, many successful teachers use incentives, or rewards, to keep students focused. Kindergarten and early elementary students might be rewarded with daily stars on a chart; some teachers allow them to choose a small prize when they have a certain number of stars. Older students respond to different incentives. They might enjoy a movie at the end of a productive week or earn a pass to have a homework assignment eliminated.

A classroom's physical space also helps shape how children learn. This is especially important in the early grades. Teachers create visual displays and stations around the room that help physically and mentally organize kids. For example, an elementary school classroom often includes a large calendar. For younger children, the teacher may also post the day's weather; older students might see notes telling when projects are due. Bulletin boards with student work and photographs can help each child feel that he or she is a meaningful part of the class. Holiday displays can guide students toward what's next, both seasonally and in their work.

CURRICULUM PLANNING

Schools expect that by the end of the year, students in each grade will have learned certain concepts and skills. However, it is often up to the teacher to ask, "What are the engaging ways we can get there, and how will students demonstrate that they've learned what I want them to learn?"

An organized teacher prepares lessons ahead of time so that students have all the information and tools they need.

To answer these questions, a teacher creates units of study within each subject area. For example, a teacher may create a unit on plants for earth science or a unit on multiplication for math. Each unit contains a series of lesson plans. A lesson plan is a description of a specific lesson. It explains what students will learn that day and how it will be presented to them. Teacher training programs include lesson plan development, and student teaching assignments allow lesson plans to be tested with children.

A well-developed lesson plan includes the title of the lesson, the time needed to complete it, and the materials required. It also states the lesson's objective, or what the student will do or know by the end. Within the plan, the teacher outlines how the lesson will progress. An innovative plan brings different skills together—science and writing, for example. Depending on the teacher's goals for the lesson, the plan may center on a group activity or individual learning. Finally, the plan explains how students will be evaluated. For example, the teacher may look at student work from the lesson to determine what students have learned and what they still need to master. This part of the teaching process is called assessment. After the lesson is completed with students, the teacher notes its successes and failures and how to improve it.

Depending on a school's procedures, the principal may require each teacher to submit lesson plans in advance on a regular basis, such as weekly. Other principals may be more informal and may just want to know that lesson plans are being prepared.

ASSESSING STUDENTS AND COMMUNICATING WITH PARENTS

Teachers need to define how each child's social and academic progress will be assessed, or judged, during the school year.

SAMPLE LESSON PLAN, THIRD GRADE SCIENCE

Here is what a sample lesson plan might look like:

BUOYANCY
Grade Level(s): Three
Subject(s): Science
Duration: Forty-five minutes
Description: Students will recognize what makes a clay ball float.
Goals: Experiment with clay to understand what makes something float.
Objectives:
1. Students will recognize the role of air in flotation.
2. Students will make changes as necessary to make something float.

Materials: Container, water, balls of clay, paper, pencils, pennies
Procedure:
1. Show the students a ball of clay. Ask them what they think will happen if it is dropped into a bowl of water.
2. Drop it in the water. Ask them why they think it sank.
3. Give each student one ball of clay. Ask them to mold the clay into a shape that will allow their clay to float.
4. Encourage students to be persistent. If time allows, students will add pennies to their "boat," counting how many pennies the boat can hold. As their boat begins to sink again, they continue to change the shape.

Assessment: After the experiment portion of the lesson, students sketch pictures of which clay shapes sank and which floated, and explain why. Discuss as a class: Did weight in the boat influence the buoyancy? How did the shape influence buoyancy? (For example, boats with higher sides kept afloat longer.)

Follow-up: This lesson can continue by using other common materials and testing their buoyancy.

They can accomplish much of this through daily grading of assignments and quizzes, as well as observation and note-taking. Students and their parents see the feedback teachers give when they check student work. Also, the patterns of

A teacher learns about a student by observing and interacting with him or her and then shares the student's progress with parents or guardians.

reward that a teacher uses to manage a class can provide each student with feedback on his or her behavior. Some teachers even ask students to participate in assessment and to judge their own progress. A teacher can also use assessments to measure what the class as a whole understands and which concepts continue to be a struggle. As a result, the teacher can tweak upcoming lessons to meet students' needs.

Parents and teachers come together for regular student-teacher conferences during the year. At this time, the regular notes a teacher takes can help paint a larger picture of the child's growth through the school year. Teachers can also help parents understand how their child manages within the social worlds of school. If successful, these conferences are a wonderful way for parents and teachers to become partners in challenging, encouraging, and helping a child.

Teachers share their assessments in a more formal way through report cards and progress reports. Learning how to write these reports in an honest yet polite and helpful way is another important skill that teachers must develop.

In schools with a supportive working environment, teachers come together to discuss the curriculum, share their best teaching ideas, or suggest ways to help a struggling student.

SCHOOL-WIDE COOPERATION

When teachers work well together, their students benefit. All of the classes in a grade can come together for special projects or learning units, for instance. Schools have also found great success when older and younger students work together, with the older students acting as guides. Older students can read to younger children or teach them how to play chess. In Maryland's Anne Arundel public school system, older and younger students work together in outdoor cleanup projects while learning about their ecosystem. Service projects of this nature can involve every grade. The first line of cooperation for a successful project is teachers, who work together to develop an idea, plan the parts of the project, and set aside time for students to participate.

TEN CHARACTERISTICS OF GOOD TEACHERS

Even after training, a good teacher draws upon his or her own personal qualities every day. Jeremy Polk, in an article for *Arts Education Policy Review*, gives his list of personal qualities that help create a good teacher:

1. Did well academically when he or she was in school.
2. Has excellent communication skills.
3. Creative.
4. Professional.
5. Understands and uses effective teaching strategies.
6. Gives students regular, helpful feedback.
7. Enjoys always learning new things.
8. Good personality.
9. Talented and knowledgeable in the subject he or she teaches.
10. Can demonstrate his or her knowledge to students.

chapter 4

WHAT QUALIFICATIONS ARE NEEDED TO TEACH?

Schools want the best teachers in their classrooms—those who encourage students and support the school. Above all else, schools are required to hire only people who have successfully trained to become a teacher. This training qualifies a person for certification, or licensure. Certification requirements exist to give teachers the tools they need to prepare, organize, deliver, and improve material in the classroom.

Public school teachers cannot teach without a valid teaching certificate, or license, in their state. This license specifies what grades one is qualified to teach. For example, a teaching certificate might state that a person is qualified to teach elementary grades one through six. Teachers in grades seven through twelve need a certificate in secondary education, with an endorsement, or approval, in their subject area. Teaching music requires its own certificate, but

this certificate typically can include all grades, kindergarten through grade twelve. Private school teachers can often teach without certification if they have a bachelor's degree.

PREPARING FOR TEACHER CERTIFICATION

How does a person get a teaching license? In order to receive one, an individual needs to complete courses in teaching and in

Teachers in training at the University of Cincinnati watch their professor give a demonstration lesson in science. High school teachers need to be certified in the subject, or content area, they would like to teach.

content areas (arts and sciences). Each state's education department specifies which courses it requires for each certificate. Teacher trainees also needs to practice teaching in a classroom, with supervision, for a certain number of hours. Finally, most states require teachers to pass one or more certification tests before they can get a license. These standardized tests require teachers to show they meet basic standards in reading, writing,

Teacher preparation programs in the United States require students to practice their skills under a working teacher's supervision. This allows them to gain real classroom experience and get feedback from someone in the field.

math, and other subjects. The exams also test knowledge of the craft of teaching.

Most aspiring teachers complete a four-year college program in teacher education that includes the courses needed for certification. Others pursue teacher education as part of a master's degree program after college. For early education and elementary school, a teacher education program includes

courses in specific subjects, such as math and English, and on teaching and learning itself. To prepare students for middle and high school certification, programs focus heavily on the subject the individual wants to teach.

As part of most programs, students need to do one or two student-teaching internships. As a student teacher, one assists in a real classroom and learns from a head teacher. A teacher education program usually places students in a classroom near the college campus. Each program has a list of cooperating teachers that have agreed (and may be trained) to work with students from the college. Some colleges allow students to complete student teaching while working at a first job in a school (as an assistant teacher, for example). Students who do this can earn money while completing their requirements. Some programs

SAMPLE CURRICULUM, TEACHER EDUCATION PROGRAM

The following are some of the courses about teaching and learning that one might take in a teacher education program. Teachers in training also take courses about teaching specific subjects, such as math or social studies.

1. **Human Growth and Learning:** This class examines how biological, social, and family influences shape a person from birth, how children and teens develop, and how schooling can influence development.

2. **Contexts of Schooling:** This class explores how schools function and fit within the larger society and how overall social views influence how schools teach.

3. **Teaching Methods:** This class introduces and compares different ways of teaching. It examines the educational research that supports various teaching techniques. It also reviews past, present, and new teaching styles.

4. **Instructional Design and Assessment:** This class looks at different ways to plan learning units and to assess, or evaluate, student performance.

5. **Seminar on Teaching:** This class brings together college or graduate students who are working as student teachers. As a group, they discuss and analyze their teaching experiences and relate them to educational theory.

even allow students to do their student teaching in a foreign country.

Student teachers are asked to demonstrate the social skills that make a good teacher. They should be able to get students to trust them and motivate them to do good work. They should show that they are aware of, and sensitive to, students' academic and cultural differences and treat each student with respect. After spending time observing their cooperating teachers, student teachers have the chance to plan and carry out their own lessons with students.

Wherever one enrolls in a teacher education program, it is important to be sure that the program is an officially approved one. Organizations such as the National Council for Accreditation of Teacher Education and the Teacher Education Accreditation Council have lists of approved programs.

APPLYING FOR TEACHER CERTIFICATION

Once a person completes the requirements for a teaching license, he or she must apply to the state department of education. This involves filling out forms, supplying proof that one has completed all of the requirements, and paying application fees. If all of the requirements are met, the department officially approves the person to teach in that state.

Aspiring teachers should make sure that a teaching program in which they are planning to enroll leads to certification in the state of their choice. Students can be more confident that they will take all the courses needed for certification if they enroll in a state-approved program. Also, students should be sure they will receive a license for the exact class they want to teach, whether it is a grade level or a special subject.

More and more states are giving all new teachers a provisional license. Teachers with this license must work in the classroom for a few years before receiving a permanent license. Even a permanent teaching license may not last the length of a teaching career and may need to be renewed. Many states now ask teachers to earn additional credits in order to renew their license. Many are even requiring teachers to earn a master's degree within the first five years of becoming a teacher.

A NATIONAL LICENSE TO TEACH

Some experienced teachers who show additional teaching skill can apply for a national teaching license through the National Board for Professional Teaching Standards. This certificate is not required to teach in any state. However, it allows teachers the option to teach in another state without going through an entire state certification process.

People should become familiar with all the routes to becoming a teacher, including programs that allow them to develop their skills or that take them to another part of the country.

After working as a teacher for some time, a teacher can apply for this license by collecting a portfolio of classroom work and taking a written test of teaching knowledge. By earning a national license, a teacher may be eligible for a higher salary. Individuals may also be able to get the certificate costs repaid. For more information on this license, contact the National Board for Professional Teaching Standards.

THE ALTERNATE ROUTE

Most states offer other ways to become a teacher, especially if one would like to teach in a geographic area or subject that has a teacher shortage. This way of training is called the alternate route. Alternate route programs allow people with college degrees in fields other than education to become certified teachers. Each state offers its own guidelines on how to complete this training.

Those taking an alternate route may begin teaching under a head teacher while they take education courses on the side. Some alternate programs approve people to teach for one or two years before they receive permanent licenses. States that desperately need teachers may give out emergency licenses, which allow people to start teaching right away.

The alternate route is helpful for a person who is older and may be working in another career, but then decides that he or she wants to become a teacher. Individuals who want to teach math and science may find more of these programs, since there is a greater need for these teachers. Also, urban schools that have a shortage of teachers may offer programs like this. Vocational education teachers may enjoy an alternate route to teaching without a college degree if they can demonstrate talent in their field. Those who are interested in taking the alternate route can contact school districts or state departments of education for more information.

chapter 5

FINDING AND STARTING A FIRST TEACHING JOB

P reparation to become a teacher starts early in one's schooling. Ideally, preparation to find one's first teaching job starts early, too. Most importantly, an aspiring teacher must narrow down what age group or grade level he or she would most like to teach.

Even with this decision made, teaching can be a very different experience from school to school and community to community. A teacher training program can help one consider the advantages and disadvantages of teaching in different types of school settings. For example, student teaching placements allow one to experience the day-to-day feel of a school and see if the setting is a good fit. Another way to gather information is to visit and interview teachers in different places. Whether rural, urban, suburban, private, public, or charter, each school setting brings a unique group of issues.

ASKING QUESTIONS

Schools, even ones in the same town, can be very different from one another. To decide where they would like to teach, teaching candidates can ask questions of each school they investigate:

What is the school's larger "culture" and vision of teaching? For example, some schools allow students to talk and be boisterous in the hallways, while others require children to walk in silent, orderly rows. A teacher will be happiest if his or her own vision is a good match with the school's.

It is also a good idea to learn more about the school community in order to understand the needs of the students. Are there many students who speak English as a second language? How many students are in special education programs? Has the community been growing or shrinking in size, and why? How does the school perform on state standardized tests, and will these tests play a large role in the school year? What is the teacher turnover rate, or how many teachers are leaving the school each year? For those who have remained, how long have they been teaching there?

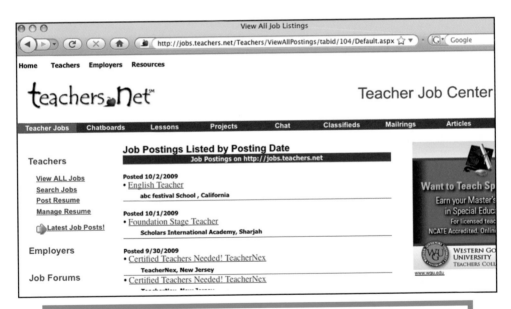

A job ad can give a basic description of a teaching position. To see if the job is a good fit, it is important to spend time with a school's students, teachers, and administrators.

Practical questions are also important. If the job requires a move to a new area, what kind of community is it? Also, it is helpful to learn about the pay and benefits that the school offers. Is the pay good for that part of the state or country?

Job fairs are excellent places to meet representatives from various school districts that need new and energetic teachers.

What benefits will be provided? Would it be possible to get more training and become an administrator, curriculum coordinator, or other specialist in the future?

GETTING INTERVIEWS

Once teaching candidates have completed course requirements and applied for state licensure (or completed the requirements for alternative certification), they are ready to begin interviewing for positions. School districts looking to collect résumés will advertise in newspapers and online, but this means the district could be flooded with hundreds of résumés. After narrowing down the search, candidates can beat the crowd by researching and writing to schools directly and expressing interest in working there. They can even call or e-mail to ask about available positions. The district staff may know of a position that is about to open up, giving an eager job hunter a spot at the head of the line. These activities will take some time, but may speed up the job search in the long run. It is also a more active approach than simply waiting with the other candidates who responded to a classified ad.

Job seekers can also ask any working teachers they know if their school has any teachers scheduled for retirement soon. After sending a résumé and cover letter to the school district's human resources department, one can also forward copies to the school principal. By doing this, a résumé is more likely to secure an interview.

If a job hunter wants to expand a search, he or she may be eligible to teach in a neighboring state, thanks to reciprocity agreements that states offer to those with certification elsewhere. Each state's reciprocity agreements are different, so one needs to check.

College career counselors have a wealth of information for teachers. They may have information on upcoming teacher job fairs. At a job fair, one can have a mini-interview with a school representative and then follow up on available positions. The college employment office may also know of state or county programs that help get new teachers into the classrooms where they are needed.

If a desirable school district has no job openings, a determined person can apply to work as a teacher's aide or substitute teacher in the targeted school district. Being present in the school can help with a job search because principals prefer to hire someone who is already a tested asset to the school.

PRESENTING: THE NEW TEACHER

When attending a job fair, meeting school administrators, or interviewing for a teaching position, it is important to already look the part of a teacher. The best bet is to dress neatly and conservatively. Learning about the school ahead of time shows that a candidate is serious about his or her career and would be a good addition to the staff. At job fairs, job hunters have only about thirty seconds to make an impression, unless the discussion turns into a sit-down interview. Either way,

FIRST-YEAR ADVICE

A teacher's first year is usually the most important. The classroom has a way of shoving theory aside and putting surprise after surprise in front of a new teacher. Seasoned teachers can offer new teachers advice to help guide them through this tricky time. Here are some tips:

- Be very, very prepared. If you are confident, students will feel confident about you.
- Create a short list of class rules about homework, bathroom breaks, etc., to help keep the class focused. For younger grades, parents can sign and return the rules.
- Seek out a more experienced teacher you admire as a mentor. This is the best guarantee that a new teacher will succeed, according to Ellen Moir of University of California, Santa Cruz's New Teacher Center.
- Observe other classrooms to see how other teachers run them.
- Communicate with the school's principal and administrators. Don't be shy.
- Share your love of learning with students.
- Be flexible.
- Keep a sense of humor.
- Find healthy ways to handle stress.
- Don't work twenty-four hours a day. Set aside some time for yourself.
- If a teacher or principal suggests you do something differently, don't be offended. He or she is probably just trying to help.
- Stay in touch with parents and stay connected to the school community.
- Most new teachers are shocked by the amount of paperwork. Find a way to manage it around your teaching.
- Set high expectations for yourself and celebrate when you reach your goals.

candidates can practice how to "sell" themselves—or sum up unique strengths—so they can share that information clearly and directly when the chance comes.

Once a new teacher is hired, he or she has a new goal: adjusting to and succeeding in the first classroom of his or her own.

THE BEGINNING TEACHER

All new jobs have a learning curve, but new teachers stand in front of a class on Day One and are asked to do the same job as experienced veterans. Instead of having the chance to ease into the profession, beginning teachers are often given the most difficult jobs or classes. New teachers are most in need at schools where more teachers have left, sometimes because

Observing an experienced teacher in action is a good way for a beginning teacher to learn.

of the challenges there. Also, new teachers must learn to teach their own classes and navigate relationships with parents, administrators, and other teachers at the same time.

How do beginning teachers increase their chances of success? Participating in a mentoring program can make a big difference. A mentoring program provides new teachers with a more experienced "coach" who teaches at a similar grade level. In such a program, new teachers can find an outlet for questions, concerns, and frustrations. The mentor can share general wisdom or suggest practical solutions to classroom challenges. Stephanie Hansen, a Chicago kindergarten teacher, told *Catalyst Chicago* magazine that her mentor helped her find an alternative to helping twenty-three students at once. "I was walking around trying to see what [one] student had written, while keeping [other students] focused on the assignment. And they all wanted my attention." Her mentor suggested she break the class into small groups that met daily, allowing her to spend time with each child in the group. It worked. "It is a much more organized workshop, and my students' writing has improved," she reported.

An experienced teacher can help put things in perspective. It can be hard for new teachers to not take things personally, such as an insult from a student. The first few years as a teacher often require strength and endurance. A mentor can keep a new teacher focused on his or her success stories instead of the problems.

As studies show how important they are, more and more schools are creating mentoring programs. Even if a school does not offer a formal mentoring program, a new teacher can still request to have a mentor.

chapter 6

THE FUTURE OF TEACHING

Teaching is a growing field. The U.S. Bureau of Labor Statistics (BLS) expects teaching positions to grow by 12 percent by 2016. This is an average rise, but there are many schools in the United States and the new jobs could total as many as 479,000 positions. Few careers will offer this number of new jobs. The number of students may or may not grow. Most new jobs will open up as today's teachers grow older and retire.

WHERE WILL THE TEACHING JOBS BE?

What teaching jobs might be a good bet? The number of teachers a school district can hire depends on how much money the town and state have in their budgets. In the coming years, there is likely to be more money for U.S. public schools as the federal government tries to raise students' skill levels. Early childhood education programs are growing because more money is being made available. Studies have found that these early programs help young children get a stronger start.

What states will have these new jobs? In what kinds of communities? Across the United States, the selection of jobs will not be the same. According to the BLS, jobs in the northeastern United States will shrink, while opportunities in the Midwest should stay the same. States in the South and Southwest—such as Nevada, Arizona, Texas, and Georgia—will likely have more jobs open to new teachers.

In all states, there are usually more available teaching positions in urban or rural communities than in suburban ones. Inner-city public schools have a harder time keeping new teachers and usually have openings each year. Urban schools especially need teachers with energy and imagination, as they often include students who are living in poverty or who have recently emigrated from other countries. In addition, as more English as a Second Language (ESL) students enter U.S. schools, schools need bilingual teachers who can teach in both English and Spanish.

In 2009, the Boston Plan for Excellence in the Public Schools found that new city teachers needed help and coaching

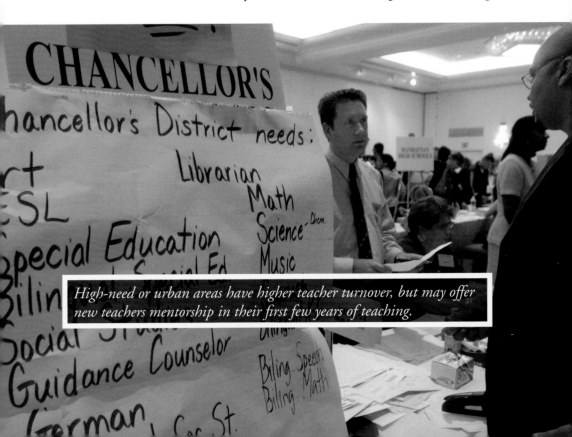

High-need or urban areas have higher teacher turnover, but may offer new teachers mentorship in their first few years of teaching.

from experienced teachers to have a good first year. Since then, Boston schools have tried to pair new teachers with a mentor. Other cities may or may not have this type of program. Those interested in working at an urban school should find out

Private and charter schools, which vary in mission and location, provide alternatives in education. For example, some focus on environmental education.

how they support their new teachers through the first few years of teaching.

In rural areas, towns have fewer residents and fewer students in school. Usually, fewer people compete for the available teaching jobs, since many of the area's young adults may have moved away. Rural schools usually pay lower salaries than suburban and urban areas, especially if the area has a lower cost of living. But for those who can move to a rural town to teach and would enjoy country life, this can be a good choice.

CHARTER AND PRIVATE SCHOOLS

Students and their families may have choices about their children's education, especially in areas where the public schools are not strong. Charter schools and private schools are the two largest categories of schools that people choose as alternatives.

A charter school is an experimental public school that is granted a charter by its state to operate independently. Charter schools are given state money to operate, but they do not have to follow the same rules as the other public schools in the area. They have the

AN INTERVIEW WITH A TEACHER

Sean Quirk is an art teacher at a New Jersey high school. After seven years in the graphic design industry, he has now taught for seven years in both private and public schools. He received his teaching certification through the alternate route program.

What do you enjoy about teaching?
I like that I am constantly learning as much as I am teaching. It's a two-way street. I learn more from the students than I teach them.

What led you to teach?
My best friend was teaching at a college. That college needed another teacher, and I already had a master's degree. When I was there, it felt magical.

How long did it take you to get certified?
It took me two and a half years to get certified. I knew I liked teaching, but I wanted to get two years under my belt before starting the process.

Did you find that was the right time to become certified?
Yes. I already had some experience. Also, unlike many of the other [certification] students, I wasn't also overwhelmed with being a first-year teacher. Later, when I was in my first year at a public high school, I learned how much of a big help that was.

What surprised you about teaching?
I didn't realize how fluid teaching would be. Teaching changes with every class you teach, and it's never the same twice.

freedom to establish their own missions, goals, and approaches to education. They are smaller, enrolling about half the students of the average public school. Most charter schools have a clear approach to teaching and look for teachers who will follow it. For example, a charter school's approach might include strict behavioral and academic discipline or an environmentally based study of all subjects. In order to keep its charter, each charter school must show the same strong grades and test scores as public schools.

Interest in charter schools has grown, and many people, especially in urban communities, are pleased that their children have this option. In New Jersey, the highest-performing urban charter schools had higher test scores in 2009 than schools in wealthy, suburban communities. Still, don't expect a huge jump in teaching jobs at charter schools just yet. The success rates are mixed, and charter schools that show low test scores or another kind of failure can be closed by the state. Charter schools may grow slowly, since states can "cap" the size of these schools. Moreover, these schools receive less state money than public schools. In 2009, ten U.S. states did not allow charter schools at all.

Private schools enroll students whose families pay tuition. While teachers in training might imagine themselves working on a large, beautiful campus with stone buildings, most private schools are smaller and found in urban areas. They may be religious in orientation—most often Catholic—and may include religious lessons as part of the students' education. Private school teachers find they have more say over how they would like to run their classroom and what they would like to teach. However, these schools do expect that teachers will support the institution's religious goals. Many private schools are able to choose the students they will accept, and so the students may be strong learners.

Overall, the number of students in all grades at private schools has grown smaller since 1990. Because they run on tuition money and donations, private schools can be hit harder by recessions, and private school teachers do not usually have the protection of tenure. Also, private schools typically offer smaller salaries than public schools and may not have the same retirement and health benefits. With smaller staffs, they also may ask teachers to be more involved in extracurricular clubs and teams.

The students of tomorrow will use technology to learn in ways that are just being tested today.

However, there are also advantages to teaching at a private school. Some private schools offer teachers discounted housing on the campus. This savings can be a big help for a young teacher. Private schools may also give a new teacher more freedom in the classroom, including more choice in what and how to teach. This can be nice for those who would like to experiment with different approaches and see what works best with their students.

THE FUTURE CLASSROOM

What skills will be needed for the classroom of the future? Computers and other technology will play a large role. Teachers are already beginning to post homework assignments and student grades with online tools. Some schools have exchanged chalkboards for whiteboards, which can be used for both traditional lessons and computer-based lessons. As more students become comfortable using computers to do their homework, the entire classroom may become more "virtual," with lessons posted online and assignments posted instead of handed in on paper. As students continue to turn to the Internet for research and study help, school libraries will expand these services. They will also help students to access information through e-books and online databases.

Each new generation of students will need excellent teachers to guide them through their education.

Some teachers find that technology helps them reach students who learn differently. Visual and auditory learners, for instance, seem to learn best when they can see and hear a lesson with multiple forms of media. Tactile (hands-on) learners may learn best when they can get out of their chairs and do a presentation or experiment. Using technology to serve different kinds of learners will probably become more common in the future. Teachers who understand how to use technology (or who are willing to be trained) will have an edge, especially at schools that are eager to try new things and involve students in new ways.

PROJECTED GROWTH AREAS FOR TEACHERS

- Preschool/early education
- Full-day kindergarten
- Mathematics
- Science (especially chemistry and physics)
- Bilingual education
- Foreign languages

It is an exciting time to be a teacher. Schools are looking for new ideas and want to challenge students in new ways. Learning is becoming more hands-on and interactive to better serve students who are hungry to understand the world around them. Teachers have a direct impact on the next generation: Their work is an investment that is not wasted. Every successful adult has at least one story about an influential teacher. And if teaching is your calling, that teacher can be you.

glossary

academics Activities related to learning subjects at a school.

administrator A person, such as a principal, who oversees a school and supervises its teachers.

alternate route A way to earn a teaching certificate for those with degrees and experience in other fields.

auditory learner Someone who learns best by hearing the information, such as in a lecture.

autism A disorder that interferes with a person's ability to communicate and relate to others.

bilingual Using two languages.

budget A set amount of money to spend.

burnout Exhaustion, and even hopelessness, that comes with a long period of overwork and stress. Teachers who suffer from burnout are more likely to leave their jobs.

certification A license that qualifies someone for a job. A teaching certification allows a person to be hired for a public school teaching job.

charter school A school founded by a group other than a town's school board, but that is supported by taxes. The school board grants the school a charter to operate independently, but is allowed to pull the charter if the school fails to meet certain standards.

curriculum The classes and academic categories offered in a school.

dyslexia A learning disability marked by difficulty with reading, writing, and spelling.

early childhood education The education a child receives in preschools or day care facilities. Early childhood education includes any schooling received before kindergarten.

emergency certification A rapidly granted teaching certificate for those without traditional teaching qualifications. Emergency certificates are used to solve teacher shortages in high-need areas or teaching categories.

English as a Second Language (ESL) Refers to an education in which, or a student for whom, English is learned after another native language.

extracurricular Relating to activities held by a school, usually after the class day is over, such as sports or clubs.

mentor A wise counselor or guide. In teaching, a mentor is an experienced, or master, teacher who helps guide a beginning teacher.

permanent license The teaching license earned in the state of one's choice once all requirements have been met. It follows a provisional teacher's license.

provisional license An initial license granted to beginning teachers. It is not permanent.

reciprocity agreement An agreement that allows a teacher who is licensed in one state to teach in another. Reciprocity agreements vary by state.

secondary The level of schooling that includes junior high school and high school, or grades seven to twelve.

standardized test A test that tries to measure how well large numbers of students in the same grade understand reading, writing, and mathematics concepts.

tenure A job benefit earned by teachers who have taught at a school for a certain number of years. Tenure protects a teacher from being fired without cause.

turnover The problem caused when trained, certified teachers quit, leaving a school to hire and train new teachers again and again.

vocational Related to skills that can be used for a career, such as car repair, cooking, carpentry, or hairstyling.

for more information

American Federation of Teachers (AFT)
555 New Jersey Ave NW
Washington, DC 20001
(202) 879-4400
Web site: http://www.aft.org
The AFT is a teachers' union with more than 1.4 million
members. Its Web site has a wealth of information about
the state of education today.

Canadian Education Association (CEA)
317 Adelaide Street West, Suite 300
Toronto, ON M5V 1P9
Canada
(416) 591-6300
Web site: http://cea-ace.ca/home.cfm
The CEA is a nonprofit that produces research on the state of
Canadian education, collects news, and collects links to
national job databases. The organization also supports
bilingual education initiatives in Canada.

Canadian Teachers Federation (CTF)
2490 Don Reid Drive
Ottawa, ON K1H 1E1
Canada
Web site: http://www.ctf-fce.ca
The trade union representing teachers in Canada, the CTF
advocates for job and school improvements and links
users to teacher job boards within the Canadian
provinces.

National Association for the Education of Young
   Children (NAEYC)
1313 L Street NW, Suite 500
Washington, DC 20005
(202) 232-8777
Web site: http://www.naeyc.org
The NAEYC focuses on educational approaches and develop-
   mental services for young children from birth through age
   eight. The association provides free resources for early
   childhood educators and offers conferences and training.

National Board for Professional Teaching Standards (NBCT)
1525 Wilson Boulevard, Suite 500
Arlington, VA 22209
(800) 228-3224
Web site: http://www.nbpts.org
This independent organization offers teacher applicants a
   National Board Certified Teacher license to assure highly
   professional teaching standards. An NBCT certification
   gives a teacher the ability to transfer his or her teaching
   license to any state in the United States.

National Center for Alternative Certification
4401A Connecticut Avenue NW, #212
Washington, DC, 20008
(888) 831-1338
Web site: http://www.teach-now.org
This organization provides information on alternate routes
   to teacher certification and guidance for alternate route
   candidates.

National Education Association (NEA)
1201 16th Street NW

Washington, DC 20036-3290
(202) 833-4000
Web site: http://www.nea.org
This teachers' union has three million U.S. public school
  teacher-members. It advocates educational issues on
  a national, state, and local level. The Web site offers
  professional development tools for teachers, such as
  classroom management tips and lesson plan ideas. The
  union offers a student membership for those enrolled in
  teacher education programs.

Teacher Education Accreditation Council (TEAC)
One Dupont Circle NW, Suite 320
Washington, DC 20036
(202) 466-7236
Web site: http://www.teac.org
A nonprofit organization, the TEAC focuses on accrediting
  and shaping colleges' undergraduate and graduate teacher
  training programs.

WEB SITES

Due to the changing nature of Internet links, Rosen Publishing
has developed an online list of Web sites related to the subject
of this book. This site is updated regularly. Please use this link
to access the list:

http://www.rosenlinks.com/ecar/teac

for further reading

Alexander, Brandy, Kimberly Persiani-Becker, and Steve Springer. *The Creative Teacher: An Encyclopedia of Ideas to Energize Your Curriculum*. New York, NY: McGraw-Hill, 2006.

Brown, Dan. *The Great Expectations School: A Rookie Year in the New Blackboard Jungle*. New York, NY: Arcade Publishing, 2008.

Edelfelt, Roy A., and Alan J. Reiman. *Careers in Education* (VGM Professional Careers Series). 4th ed. Chicago, IL: VGM Career Books, 2004.

Esquith, Rafe. *Teach Like Your Hair's on Fire: The Methods and Madness Inside Room 56*. New York, NY: Penguin, 2007.

Fine, Janet. *Opportunities in Teaching Careers*. Revised edition. New York, NY: McGraw-Hill, 2005.

Kozol, Jonathan. *Letters to a Young Teacher*. New York, NY: Three Rivers Press, 2008.

Loewen, James W. *Lies My Teacher Told Me: Everything Your American History Textbook Got Wrong*. New York, NY: Touchstone, 2007.

Mandel, Scott M. *The New Teacher Toolbox: Proven Tips and Strategies for a Great First Year*. 2nd ed. Thousand Oaks, CA: Corwin, 2009.

McCourt, Frank. *Teacher Man*. New York, NY: Scribner, 2005.

Perlstein, Linda. *Tested: One American School Struggles to Make the Grade*. Austin, TX: Holt, 2008.

Thompson, Julia G. *First Year Teacher's Survival Guide: Ready-to-Use Strategies, Tools & Activities for Meeting the Challenges of Each School Day* (J-B Ed: Survival Guides). 2nd ed. Hoboken, NJ: Jossey-Bass, 2007.

bibliography

American Federation of Teachers. "Becoming a Teacher." June 2008. Retrieved August 14, 2009 (http://www.aft. org/tools4teachers/career/becoming.htm).

Bodilly, Susan J., and Jennifer Li. "The Role of Charter Schools in Improving Education." Rand Corporation, 2009. Retrieved August 4, 2009 (http://www.rand.org/ pubs/research_briefs/RB9428).

California Teachers Association. "Promoting Teacher Quality: Recommendations from the California Teachers Association." October 19, 2007. Retrieved August 10, 2009 (http://www.edsource.org/reform_ convening.html#briefs).

Cromwell, Sharon. "Where Does Sixth Grade Belong?" *Education World*, 2005. Retrieved August 18, 2009 (http:// www.educationworld.com/a_issues/issues/issues030. shtml).

Friedman, Alexi. "Urban Charter Schools in New Jersey Are Excelling." New Jersey On-Line LLC, March 22, 2009. Retrieved August 4, 2009 (http://www.nj.com/ news/index.ssf/2009/03/urban_charter_schools_in_ new_j.html).

Harris Interactive. "MetLife Survey of the American Teacher: Past, Present and Future. A Survey of Teachers, Principals and Students." October 2008. Retrieved August 14, 2009 (http://www.eric.ed.gov).

Holland, Sally. "Despite Push, Year-Round Schools Get Mixed Grades." CNN.com, September 10, 2009. Retrieved September 10, 2009 (http://www.cnn.com/ 2009/US/09/04/us.year.round.schools/index.html).

Mattioli, Dana. "A Hard Lesson for Teachers."
    Wall Street Journal, August 11, 2009. Retrieved
    August 12, 2009 (http://online.wsj.com/article/
    SB10001424052970203612504574342530405184284.html).

Moir, Ellen. "The New Teacher Project: Support for
    Educators During Their First Years." Edutopia.org,
    October 1, 2000. Retrieved August 20, 2009 (http://www.
    edutopia.org/supporting-new-teachers).

MuniNetGuide. "Recession Exerts Pressure on Public School
    District Budgets." July 30, 2009. Retrieved August 6,
    2009 (http://www.muninetguide.com/articles/recession-
    exerts-pressure-on-public-school-distr-328.php).

National Alliance for Public Charter Schools. "Public
    Charter School Dashboard 2009." June 19, 2009.
    Retrieved August 6, 2009 (http://www.
    publiccharters.org/node/984).

Reeger, Jennifer. "Kindergarten: It's Academic." *Tribune-
    Review*, April 18, 2005. Retrieved August 14, 2009
    (http://www.pittsburghlive.com/x/
    pittsburghtrib/s_325248.html).

Robelen, Erik W. "State Picture on Charter Caps Still Mixed."
    Education Week, August 11, 2009. Retrieved August 5,
    2009 (http://www.edweek.org).

Rodriguez, Victor Javier. "Minority Teacher Shortage Plagues
    Region, Nation." *SEDL Letter*, Vol. XII No. 2, December
    2000. Retrieved August 15, 2009 (http://www.sedl.org/
    pubs/sedletter/v12n02/7.html).

Scholastic Administrator. "Universal Preschool: Is It
    Necessary?" September/October 2009. Retrieved
    September 5, 2009 (http://www2.scholastic.com/browse/
    article.jsp?id=3752507).

Stengel, Richard. "Arne Duncan: The Apostle of
    Reform." *Time*, April 27, 2009. Retrieved August 10,

2009 (http://www.time.com/time/politics/article/
0,8599,1891473,00.html).

U.S. Department of Education. "Evaluation of the Public
Charter Schools Program: Final Report: Executive
Summary." November 19, 2004. Retrieved August 4,
2009 (http://www.ed.gov/rschstat/eval/choice/
pcsp-final/finalreport.pdf).

U.S. Department of Education, National Center for
Education Statistics. "A Brief Profile of America's Private
Schools." 2003. Retrieved August 10, 2009 (http://nces.
ed.gov/pubs2003/2003417.pdf).

Weiss, Anna. "Summer Break Not Really a Break for
Teachers." *The Philadelphia Public School Notebook*,
August 25, 2009. Retrieved August 30, 2009 (http://
www.thenotebook.org/blog/091616/summer-break-
not-really-break-teachers).

Williams, Debra. "Coaches Keep Rookie Teachers on Track."
Catalyst Chicago, April 2008. Retrieved August 20,
2009 (http://www.catalyst-chicago.org/news/index.
php?item=2399&cat=30).

index

ABOUT THE AUTHOR

Annalise Silivanch has always wanted to be a teacher and now teaches college students as area chair for the Department of Humanities at the University of Phoenix in Jersey City, New Jersey. Her college instruction experience includes coaching students to set personal and professional goals for themselves.

PHOTO CREDITS

Designer: Matthew Cauli; Editor: Andrea Sclarow; Photo Researcher: Marty Levick